D1383259

What's Awake?

Barn Owls

Patricia Whitehouse

Heinemann Library
Chicago, Illinois

www.heinemannraintree.com
Visit our website to find out more information about Heinemann-Raintree books.

To order:

Phone 888-454-2279
Visit www.heinemannraintree.com to browse our catalog and order online.

Edited by Adrian Vigliano and Diyan Leake
Designed by Joanna Hinton-Malivoire
Picture research by Tracy Cummins
Originated by Chroma Graphics (Overseas) Pte Ltd
Printed in China by South China Printing Company Ltd

13 12 11 10
10 9 8 7 6 5 4 3 2 1

New edition ISBNs: 978 1 4329 2590 1 (hardback)
978 1 4329 2599 4 (paperback)

The Library of Congress has cataloged the first edition as follows:
Whitehouse, Patricia, 1958
Barn owls / Patricia Whitehouse.
p. cm. — (What's awake)
Includes index.
Summary: Describes the physical characteristics, behavior, and habitat of barn owls.
ISBN: 1 58810 877 5 (HC), 1 40340 624 3 (Pbk.)
1. Barn owls—Juvenile literature. [1. barn owls.] I. Title.
QL696.S85 W55 2002
598.9'7—dc21

2001006389

Acknowledgments

The author and publisher are grateful to the following for permission to reproduce copyright material: agefotostock p. **19** (© Gary Smith); Corbis p. **13** (© zefa/Helmut Heintges); Getty Images pp. **12** (© Christopher Robbins), **17** (© Christopher Robbins), **21** (© Joe McDonald); istockphoto pp. **10** (© Inga Brennan - Photography & Design), **16** (© John Pitcher), **23f** (© Andrew_Howe); National Geographic p. **6** (© Minden Pictures/Micahel Durham); Photo Researchers pp. **22** (© Stephen Dalton), **23e** (© Stephen Dalton); Photolibrary pp. **9** (© Juniors Bildarchiv), **11** (© Dennis Green); Photoshot pp. **14** (© Imagebroker.net), **15** (© NHPA); Shutterstock pp. **4** (© Dainis Derics), **5** (© Joanne Harris and Daniel Bubnich), **8** (© Daniel Hebert), **23a** (© Yanik Chauvin), **23b** (© Nick Biemans), **23c** (© Newton Page), **23d** (© Martin Wall); Visual Unlimited pp. **7** (Joe McDonald), **18a** (© Robert Barber), **18b** (© Robert Barber), **20** (S. Maslowski).

Cover photograph reproduced with permission of Nature Picture Library (© Mike Read). Back cover photograph of an owl's beak reproduced with permission of Shutterstock (© Yanik Chauvin) and photograph of an owl's wing reproduced with permission of Shutterstock (© Nick Biemans).

Every effort has been made to contact copyright holders of any material reproduced in this book. Any omissions will be rectified in subsequent printings if notice is given to the publisher.

CAUTION: Remind children that it is not a good idea to handle wild animals. Children should wash their hands with soap and water after they touch any animal.

Contents

Some words are shown in bold, **like this**. You can find them in the picture glossary on page 23.

What's Awake?

Some animals are awake when you go to sleep.

Animals that stay awake at night are **nocturnal**.

Barn owls are awake at night.

What Are Barn Owls?

Barn owls are birds.

Birds have **feathers** and wings.

Birds lay eggs.

Baby birds come out of the eggs.

What Do Barn Owls Look Like?

Barn owls have white **feathers** on their faces.

Their other feathers can be gray or brown.

Barn owls have short, sharp **beaks**.

They have sharp **talons**.

Where Do Barn Owls Live?

Barn owls live in dark places.

They build **nests** in caves or holes in trees.

They build nests in barns.

They build nests in piles of hay, too.

What Do Barn Owls Do at Night?

Barn owls look for food at night.

They fly over fields.

Barn owls find something to eat.

They grab it with their **talons**.

What Do Barn Owls Eat?

Barn owls eat small **nocturnal** animals.

Barn owls eat mice.

Barn owls also eat **voles**.

A vole looks like a mouse with a short tail.

What Do Barn Owls Sound Like?

Barn owls make a loud hissing noise.

They do not hoot like other owls.

A barn owl's call might wake you up at night.

How Are Barn Owls Special?

A barn owl can turn its head to see what is behind it.

It can hear very well, too.

A barn owl can hear better than it sees.

It uses its hearing to find food.

Where Do Barn Owls Go During the Day?

In the morning, barn owls go back to their **nests**.

They sleep until it is dark again.

Owl Map

Picture Glossary

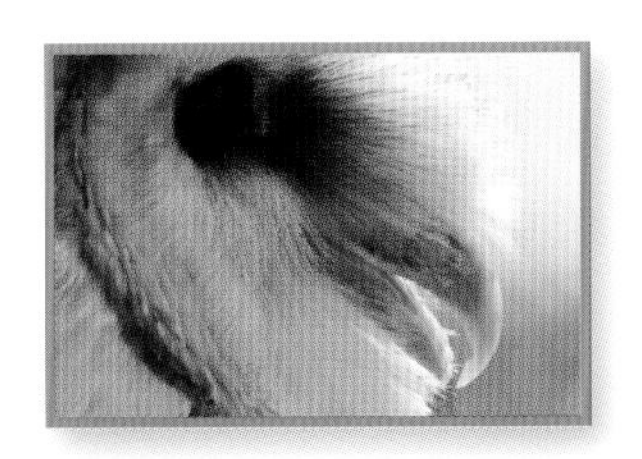

beak sharp nose and mouth of a bird

feather one of the long, light things that cover a bird's body

nest place that birds make to rest and have their families

nocturnal awake at night

talons sharp curved toes on a bird's feet

vole small animal like a mouse with a short tail

Index

Note to Parents and Teachers

Reading for information is an important part of a child's literacy development. Learning begins with a question about something. Help children think of themselves as investigators and researchers by encouraging their questions about the world around them. In this book, the animal is identified as a bird. A bird by definition is an animal that is covered with feathers and has wings. Point out the fact that there are many familiar birds in the world around us and help the children to identify them.